WITHDRAWN

D0392253

Character Values

I Have
Self-Respect

by Sarah L. Schuette

Consulting Editor: Gail Saunders-Smith, PhD

Consultant: Madonna Murphy, PhD
Professor of Education, University of St. Francis, Joliet, Illinois
Author, *Character Education in America's Blue Ribbon Schools*

Capstone
press®
Mankato, Minnesota

Pebble Books are published by Capstone Press,
P.O. Box 669, 151 Good Counsel Drive, Mankato, Minnesota 56002.
www.capstonepress.com

Copyright © 2007 Capstone Press. All rights reserved.
No part of this publication may be reproduced in whole or in part, or stored in a
retrieval system, or transmitted in any form or by any means, electronic, mechanical,
photocopying, recording, or otherwise, without written permission of the publisher.
For information regarding permission, write to Capstone Press,
151 Good Counsel Drive, P.O. Box 669, Dept. R, Mankato, Minnesota 56002.
Printed in the United States of America

1 2 3 4 5 6 11 10 09 08 07 06

Library of Congress Cataloging-in-Publication Data
Schuette, Sarah L., 1976–
  I have self-respect / by Sarah L. Schuette.
    p. cm.—(Character values)
  Summary: "Simple text and photographs help define self-respect"—Provided
by publisher.
  Includes bibliographical references and index.
  ISBN-13: 978-0-7368-6337-7 (hardcover)
  ISBN-10: 0-7368-6337-0 (hardcover)
  1. Self-esteem—Juvenile literature. 2. Character—Juvenile literature. I. Title.
II. Series.
BJ1533.S3S33 2007
158.1—dc22
                                                                          2006000518

Note to Parents and Teachers

The Character Values set supports national social studies standards
for units on individual development and identity. This book
describes self-respect and illustrates ways students can show
self-respect. The photographs support early readers in
understanding the text. The repetition of words and phrases helps
early readers learn new words. This book also introduces early
readers to subject-specific vocabulary words, which are defined in
the Glossary. Early readers may need assistance to read some words
and to use the Table of Contents, Glossary, Read More, Internet
Sites, and Index sections of the book.

Table of Contents

Self-Respect

I have self-respect.

I am unique.

I like who I am.

I am happy and kind.
I try to act that way
around other people.

At Home

I respect my body.
I keep it clean
and looking nice.

I take care
of what I have.
I fold my clothes
and put them away.

I respect my feelings.
I talk to my dad
when I am sad.

At School

I show a positive attitude.
I keep trying even when
it is hard.

I develop my talents.
I do the best I can.

18

I know I do not
have to be perfect.
It's okay
to make mistakes.

Feeling Good

I am proud of myself.
Nobody else
is just like me.

Glossary

attitude—the way you feel; people with positive attitudes are happy and fun to be around.

develop—to work on and to get better at something

respect—to show you care; self-respect is caring about yourself.

talent—something that you can do well and are good at

unique—one of a kind

Read More

Johansen, Heidi Leigh. *What I Look Like When I Am Happy.* Let's Look at Feelings. New York: PowerStart Press, 2004.

Powell, Jillian. *Self-Esteem.* It's Your Health. North Mankato, Minn.: Smart Apple Media, 2006.

Internet Sites

FactHound offers a safe, fun way to find Internet sites related to this book. All of the sites on FactHound have been researched by our staff.

Here's how:

1. Visit *www.facthound.com*

2. Choose your grade level.

3. Type in this book ID **0736863370** for age-appropriate sites. You may also browse subjects by clicking on letters, or by clicking on pictures and words.

4. Click on the **Fetch It** button.

FactHound will fetch the best sites for you!

Index

Word Count: 112
Early-Intervention Level: 14

Editorial Credits
Amber Bannerman, editor; Jennifer Bergstrom, set designer and illustrator; Ted Williams, book designer

Photo Credits
Capstone Press/Karon Dubke, all

The author dedicates this book to her neighbors, Ivan and Doreen Lehnert of Belle Plaine, Minnesota.